SANDSTORM

by Peter Millett

illustrated by Giorgio Bacchin

CAMBRIDGE
UNIVERSITY PRESS

UCL
Institute of Education

~ CHAPTER 1 ~

Shan and Jia were riding ponies
with their mum and dad.

'Can we ride faster?' Jia asked her parents.

'Yeah, your horses are too slow!' grinned Shan.

'Okay,' Mum said. 'But please be careful.'

'Yes,' said Dad. 'Don't go too far ahead of us or you will get lost.'

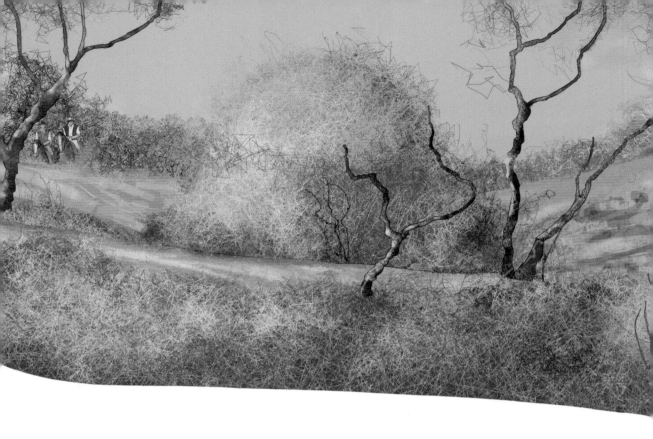

Shan and Jia rode on ahead
and soon they were in a hot valley.

They stopped to rest. Shan had a drink of water.

Jia looked round.
'Hey, can you see Mum and Dad?' she asked.

'Yep,' Shan smiled.
'But they are a long way behind us.'

A moment later, Shan's smile turned into a frown.

'Oh no! Look at that!' he yelled,
pointing to his left.

A cloud of dust rolled quickly towards
Shan and Jia.

CHAPTER 2

'It's a sandstorm!' Shan cried.

Jia gasped. 'What do we do?' she asked.

Their horses lifted their heads and snorted.

'We have to stay calm,' Shan said quietly.

'If we panic, our horses will panic, too.'

Shan and Jia rode up to a tree and stopped.

They jumped down and Shan tied the horses
to some branches.

As the storm grew nearer, Shan pulled
his sweatshirt out of his backpack.

'We need to cover our faces right now,'
he said, winding the sweatshirt
around his nose and mouth.

Jia pulled out her shawl and covered her face.

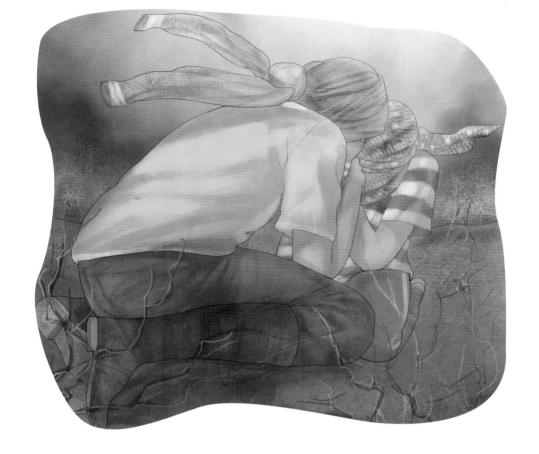

A moment later, the dust cloud swept around them like a wave.

Sand blasted Shan and Jia.

'Curl up like a ball,' Shan said.
'And close your eyes!'

Jia did as Shan told her and curled up on the ground.

The horses closed their eyelids
and dipped their noses into the storm.

The dust raced over Shan and Jia's heads.

The cloud of dust covered them,
and the hot flying sand stung them.

11

The sky turned black. It was darker than the middle of the night.

'Ouch,' Jia cried, as something hard hit her.

'It's hail,' Shan shouted from under his sweatshirt.

Jia was frightened.

'When can I open my eyes?' she asked.

'Not now!' Shan shouted. 'You must keep your eyes shut or the sand will blind you.'

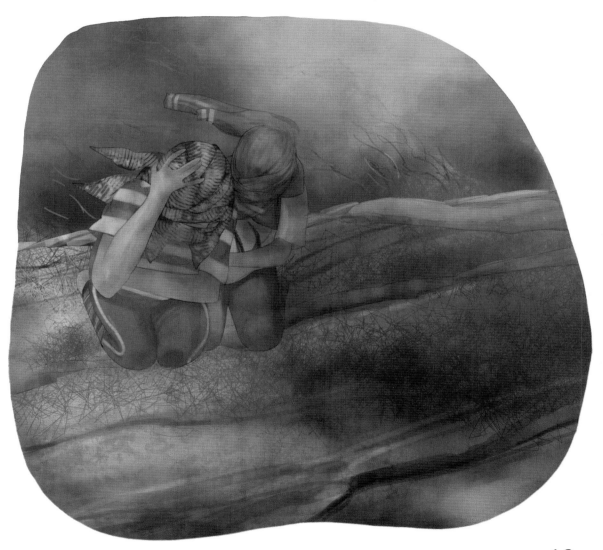

'But how will we find Mum and Dad
if we keep our eyes closed?' asked Jia.

'Don't worry, Jia, they'll find us!' said Shan.

The horses shook and stamped their feet.
They were frightened, too.

~ CHAPTER 3 ~

Then, all of a sudden, the hail stopped and everything went quiet.

'Can I open my eyes now?' Jia asked.

'Not yet,' Shan said. 'Wait a bit longer.'

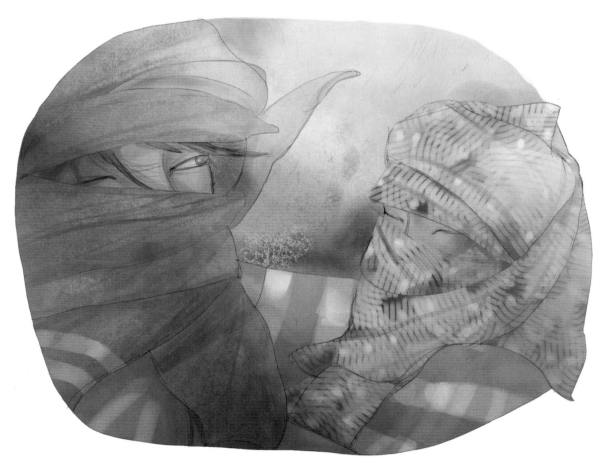

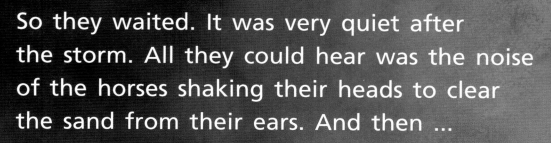

So they waited. It was very quiet after
the storm. All they could hear was the noise
of the horses shaking their heads to clear
the sand from their ears. And then ...

'Kids! Are you all right?' shouted a distant voice.

'Is that you, Dad?'
Shan shouted.

Then the sands lifted into the sky and the sun came out.

Shan peeped out from under his sweatshirt. 'The storm has gone,' he said. 'You can open your eyes now, Jia.'

Jia uncovered her face. She looked up at the sky and smiled.

'I hope the horses are okay,' she said. Jia went over to where Shan had tied them to the tree.

Both horses looked calm.

'Oh, they're fine,' she said, rubbing sand from their heads.

Shan patted the horses. 'You were both so brave,' he told them.

'Kids, we're over here,' Mum and Dad shouted.

Jia and Shan turned to see their parents.

'You're safe!' Dad said. 'We are so proud of you. You stayed calm. You curled up like a ball. You did everything right.'

Mum smiled and hugged Shan and Jia.

'It's time to go home,' she said.

'Do you want to ride ahead of us again?' said Dad.

'No thanks,' Shan replied. 'We want to take the slow and safe way home now!'

SANDSTORM! 🐀 PETER MILLETT

Teaching notes written by Sue Bodman and Glen Franklin

Using this book

Developing reading comprehension

This exciting adventure story builds tension over a sequence of time and building towards a resolution. The text provides opportunity to consider characterisation and motive, and the implications of action. The book is written in short chapters to support sustained reading.

Grammar and sentence structure

- Sentences are longer and more complex, using a range of causal connectives to sustain more than one idea.
- Variation in sentence structure for dramatic effect (e.g. page 20).

Word meaning and spelling

- Vocabulary choices to demonstrate heightened tension and change of mood (e.g. 'grinned' 'gasped' 'frowned').
- The spelling of past tense 'ed' verbs, exploring conventions for doubling consonants (e.g. 'hugged', 'grinned') and 'y' to 'ied' (such as 'replied').

Curriculum links

Geography – Work on climatic conditions in desert regions. Compare with other weather phenomena such as snowstorms, tornados, etc.

PSHE – Theme of staying safe. Children could write warning posters or safety leaflets, particularly related to risks in their own context.

Learning outcomes

Children can:

- identify and describe characters
- read silently or quietly at a more rapid pace
- take note of punctuation and use it to keep track of longer sentences
- solve most unfamiliar words using appropriate word-reading strategies.

A guided reading lesson

Book Introduction

Give each child a copy of the book. Ask them to read the front cover, the blurb and the first chapter (pages 2-5). N.B. This could be done prior to the guided reading session as an independent activity.

Orientation

Have the children retell what has happened in the first chapter. Draw out what they know already of the characters and the setting. Go to page 3 and read together Mum and Dad's warning to the children. Ask: *Do you think the children listened to their parents warning? Why not? Look on page 5. What has Shan seen? How do we know he was worried?* Look for the information in the text, identifying the verbs that indicate this. Ask the children to predict what they think will happen. Call upon the title, blurb and information from this first chapter to support their predictions.

Preparation

Say: *This book is written in chapters. We've talked about the first chapter. Now you are going to read chapter 2. First I want you to quickly look through the chapter by yourself (pages 6 – 15) then turn to your partner and discuss what you can see happening to Shan and Jia. Bring the group back together and*